Business Essentials for SMEs

By Brydon Davidson

Tools to Start, Grow, and Sustain Your Business
for Better Profits and Easy Tax Management

Published by: Infinite Possibilities Ltd
Unit 14, Lynden Court,
Chartwell, Hamilton, New Zealand
Cover Design by Daniela Catucci

ISBN: 978-0-473-38372-5
Printed by CreateSpace
Cover Design by Catucci Design

CONTENTS

Introduction - Who is this book for? 4

Part One - Making Your Business Work for You 7

1: RULE #1: RELEVANCE...................................11

2: RULE #2: PRICING 15

3: RULE #3: PROFIT 19

4: Breaking the rules....................................25

Part Two - How to Grow Your Business 27

5: An Accountant's perspective.....................................29

6: Is it really so hard to grow your business? 33

7: Changing times call for new ways of thinking 39

8: Building the right conditions for growth 43

9: What do you hope to achieve from growing?...........47

10: Ten ways to nurture growth...................................51

11: Sustaining growth...57

Part Three - Managing Your Tax Easily 61

13: Accountants and tax..63

14: Timing is everything 69

15: The best way to plan for tax....................................77

16: Getting help from your accountant 83
Conclusion 87

Next Steps..88

About Brydon Davidson..89

Infinite Possibilities..91

A note of thanks from the author 95

Introduction - Who is this book for?

This is for you if:

- None of the usual strategies or tools have worked to run your business the way you want;
- You've ever felt lost and unsure about what you're doing when it comes to running your business;
- You're starting a business (or about to start your business) and not sure what you should be doing;
- You want a proven way to run your business that allows you to reach your goals no matter what.

I've divided this book into three specific areas that are of most concern to entrepreneurs.

In Part One you'll discover:
- The three golden rules to running any business;
- Seven things to consider to be more relevant to your customers;

- Five things to consider to make sure you're selling your products/services at a price your customers are willing to pay;
- Twelve things to consider to make sure you're selling your products/services for enough to make a profit;
- And when it's okay and not okay to break the rules.

In Part Two, you'll discover the specific things you need to focus on to assist your growth in your business. These include:

- The four mistaken beliefs that hold most entrepreneurs back
- The 10 levers for growth
- How to build resilience in your business to sustain your growth
- How to identify when you are growing too fast and how to work through the symptoms of rapid growth.

In Part Three you'll learn more about your tax planning essentials, including:

- A simply and proven way to always pay your tax on time
- How important it is to stay on the right side of the Tax Man
- Why timing is everything in terms of tax management
- Early signs to help identify when your business is in trouble

WARNING – If you decide to read this, you'll be able to run your business, no question about it. But you need to know that getting from where you are now to where you want to be will be very challenging. The Truth is *"Words remain words unless they are acted upon and implemented"*. If you're not ready to actually do something with what I'm sharing with you, then you should save yourself some time and stop reading this book right now. Give it to someone else who is ready to change instead. If you are ready to do something then read on …

Part One

Making Your Business Work for You

Last year I decided that it was time to help teach my daughter her first lesson about running a business. She was six years old and we had more apples than we could eat or need to freeze for apple pies in winters. I figured it was a good opportunity to teach her some basics of starting a business and making a bit of extra pocket money in the process.

Without a lot of forethought – after all she is only six - I sat down with her to share some of the basic rules of being in business. I had never thought about this before but I figured how hard could that be? Really? I'm an accountant. I started and run my own business that has supported my family for the last six years. I work with business owners helping them do better in their businesses. This should be easy. Turns out, not so much!!

As I attempted to teach my daughter about running a business, I realised I couldn't do it the conventional way because I was constantly having to explain the words and concepts I was trying to use. For those of you who have had children, you will understand that it's pointless trying to explain too many things at one time because they're a bit like Dory (the fish in Finding Nemo) and get easily distracted by more interesting things ("ohhh look … sand … I like sand …" and off she goes).

I quickly understood that the rules of running a business should be the same whether I am explaining them to my six year old daughter, my clients, or anyone else. They should be so simple that anyone gets it - the *first* time. They shouldn't be bogged down in business terms that need further explaining. And they have to be true no matter what business you're in, how big your business is, or where you run your business from. Whether you are setting up your first apple/lemon/melon stall with your dad at the end of your driveway, or you are Coca Cola selling drinks around the world.

Bearing this in mind, I came up with these three golden rules to running any business:

1. You need to sell a product/service people want to buy.
2. You need to sell your product/service at a price your customers are willing to pay.
3. You need to sell your product/service for enough to make a profit.

Respect these three rules and your business should be fine (hopefully better than fine). Break these rules and you're going to find your business in trouble sooner or later.

I can already hear some of you asking "What about the other things like finance, marketing, employees, the tax man, administration, sales ….? You know, all those things they talk about in books and on the internet about running a business". They're important too, but as I will explain, they're not rules you need to listen to when you're running a business – they're more like parts of a rule than a rule themselves.

1

RULE #1: RELEVANCE

You need to sell something people want to buy!

In the 1970's and 1980's Sony was at war with JVC in what was known as the videotape format war (for those of you too young to have been around at that time, videotapes were the video equivalent of tape decks for music before they were replaced with CD's). Sony was first to market with its Betamax Video Cassette Recorder (VCR) in 1975 and JVC's VHS VCR followed in 1976.

The ultimate winner was decided by the two things – one of those things was the recording time (think relevance) of their VCR. When it came to recording time, Sony's Betamax could only record for 60 minutes. JVC's VHS could record 120 minutes. This meant most feature films could be recorded on the VHS format without a tape change. Betamax couldn't do that.

Sony's Betamax didn't take into account what consumers wanted. By 1981, Sony had dropped from 100% market share in 1975 to just 25%. And in 1988 Sony started selling VHS format VCR players. They ended up learning an expensive lesson about trying to sell something people didn't want. ***It doesn't matter how good your marketing is, when you are selling something customers don't want, you're going to lose.***

What happens when you are relevant to your customer?

- Your customers know what you, your products and/or services can do for them.
- Your customers know where to find you.
- You have new customers showing up all the time.
- Your customers tend to stick around.
- You have plenty of customers.
- Sales increase.

What happens when you are not relevant to your customers?

- Your customers don't understand (or have trouble understanding) what you, your products and/or services can do for them.
- Your customers have trouble finding you or can't find you at all.
- You have little or no new leads/prospects.
- Your customers are leaving you.
- You don't have enough customers.
- Sales Decrease.

How can you become more relevant to your customers?

- **Know your customers** – the more you know about your customer (e.g. age, gender, income, where are they, where they go, what they do, what their pain points are, what they need, what's important to them) then the more you understand them and their needs … so you can make sure you meet them.

- **Location** – you wouldn't go fishing for fish in the desert, you'd fish where the fish are (in the water and where they like to feed). Know where your customers are, where they go, and where they want to be. That way you can be there too. Your location doesn't just include your physical office/store – think about where you should 'put' your website as well.

- **Competition** – know who your competitors are. Know why your customers use them and not you and do something about it. Learn from your competitors' mistakes, use what works for them, and avoid the things they do that don't work.

- **Purpose** - Why are you 'here' (in business)? What do you stand for? Your customer wants to know why they should do business with you. Stand out from your competitors so your customers can find you easier. Don't be part of the *loudest* or *brightest* or *most obnoxious* just to stand out – stand out by choosing a reason that's important to your customers (because you know them, right?). Points of difference might be price, services, quality, range, or value.

- **Products/Services** – Much like your business, your products/services should be important to your customers. They should meet a need, want or desire your customer your customer has.

- **Education** - Your product or service might be obvious in which case there is little education needed. It might not be obvious in which case you'll need to consider adding an education aspect to what you're selling. For example, no one really knew they 'needed' a smartphone until they knew what it could do,

- **Marketing** – When you go fishing, you wouldn't use my shoe as bait for fish. You'd find out what kind of bait the fish *you're* fishing for like, and use that. Communicate your business's point of difference in a clear, concise and compelling way, and use your customers' language – don't talk Martian if they live on the moon. Limit the industry jargon as much as possible.

- **Surveys/Feedback** – create a dialogue with your customers to find out if you need to do anything to become more relevant. Customers don't always know what they want so instead, try asking your customers what challenges or obstacles are getting in their way when it comes to 'whatever it is you offer'. Then find ways to deliver on that (obviously choosing the ones most of your customers want first).

2

RULE #2: PRICING

You need to sell it at a price customers are willing to pay.

Going back to the Sony Betamax versus JVC VHS video format war, another factor that determined the winner and the loser was the price points of the VCR.

Sony's Betamax was a superior recording format over JVC's VHS due to resolution, slightly superior sound, and a more stable image; Betamax recorders were also of higher quality construction. The higher quality meant the Betamax was more expensive than the VHS video cassette recorder. Unfortunately for Sony, it turned out that the higher quality differences weren't enough to make up for the higher price tag, and they also didn't make up for Sony's Betamax's shorter recording time.

Consumers wanted an *affordable* VCR and a JVC VHS often cost hundreds of dollars less than a Sony Betamax. As Sony learned, it's no good selling something your customers want if they're not prepared to pay for it.

What happens if you sell what you make/offer at a price your customers are willing to pay?
- You'll be more likely to get customers purchasing whatever it is you're selling.
- Your customers will spend more each time they buy from you and/or they'll be back to buy from you more often.
- Your customers will be more willing to pay what they owe you.
- Your customers are far less likely to provide discounts.
- Sales increase.
- Gross Profit increases.
- Costs can decrease.
- You'll be better able to cover costs of producing your product/service.

What happens when you don't sell your product or service at a price your customers are willing to pay
- Customers are showing up in your office/store but you're just not getting the sale.
- Your customers aren't buying from you as much as they used to – that's either per sale and/or number of sales in a year.
- You're having trouble collecting the money from your customers.
- You're having to discount more to get the sale.

- You're being asked to drop your prices or if you'll give discounts all the time.
- Falling sales.
- Falling gross profit.
- Increasing costs.
- It's harder to cover costs of producing your product/service.

How can you make sure you're selling your products/services at a price your customers are willing to pay?

- **Value** - Your customer isn't interested in your product or service, they are interested in what your product or service *can do for them* (this is the value your product/service gives them). Do you understand what problems your product/service solves for your customer? Don't just think about how much money your product/service can give your customer – think about how much time it might save them, or how much stress it could remove too. Once you know the true value (in terms of time, money and stress) of what you're selling then you can easily price accordingly.

- **Price** – Ultimately the price you sell to your customer is the highest amount your customer would accept before they say "no thanks". The problem is you aren't a mind reader so you won't know – if they say yes too quickly then you may be priced too low. If they say no then you may be too high (or the customer doesn't understand the value you're providing). Understand the REAL value of what you're offering your customer to help you find the right price.

- **Marketing** – Communicate the value your product/service gives your customer in a clear, concise and compelling way. Use your customers' language.   If you're not sure, then ask your customer. Give your customers two or three (no more) options based on value so they feel in control of their purchasing decision – it also gives you some room to move when it comes to pricing objections.

- **Discounting** – Simply put … DON'T!!! Consider adding value instead. Or incentivise. Discounts are perceived as 'cheap' and unless they are planned and for specific time frames, they normally lead to a discount war and a race to the bottom for everyone.

- **Credit terms** – Do you want to give your customers credit terms? Are credit terms something your customers would value? Giving credit terms to your customers means you act like a bank. And just like a bank you will need terms of trade to cover the terms of repayment. And never forget – a sale ends once the money is in your bank account because you can't spend a loan – *so make sure you get paid*.

3

RULE #3: PROFIT

You need to sell your service/product for more than it costs you.

The number one rule of being in business: if the cost of the product/service you sell is greater than what your customer pays you for your product/service then you will make a loss. That loss must be covered from somewhere – your own funds, savings, previous profits, or loans. If allowed to continue too long, there may be nothing to cover the losses and at that point the business will be bankrupt because it won't be able to pay the taxman, suppliers, banks, employees, not to mention your own costs of living.

Businesses tend to end up selling their products/services for less than it costs them usually for one of these reasons:
1. They start to find themselves struggling to sell to customers (this can be the result of becoming less relevant, more competition, or customers no longer

willing to pay what they used to) so the business owner starts offering discounts, and/or they start dropping prices just to get the sales. If allowed to continue, sooner or later the sales will end up lower than costs.
2. Prices invariably go up over time. So unless business owners review their costs, or look for newer, better, more efficient ways to do business to keep costs down, the costs relating to the product/service a business provides will end up increasing too. If the costs of a business are increasing, and a business does not in turn review its sale price to customers accordingly, sooner or later its costs will be greater than its sales.

It is important to note that selling more when your costs are greater than your sales will never help you. In fact it will hurt you more and result in your business failing that much faster and more spectacularly. Businesses need to continually review their costs and sales to make sure they aren't making losses.

What happens when you sell what you make/offer for enough to make a profit?
- Sales will be greater than costs.
- You can pay your suppliers, employees, your loans, and your taxes.
- You make a profit.

What happens when you don't sell what you make/offer for enough to make a profit?
- You end up not having enough money to pay your loans, your suppliers, your employees, your taxes to the Government.
- Costs are greater than sales.

- You start making losses that may be non-recoverable.

How do you make sure you're selling your products or services for enough to make a profit?

Cash is KING!! – There is an old saying: "sales are vanity, profit is sanity, and cash is reality". Remember this – it's no good selling products/services at one price but banking a lesser amount (due to discounts, rebates, and bad debts/non-payment). You can't spend debts – you need cash to pay your bills. Many a 'successful' business has failed due to large sales growth and ignoring their cash flow.

Lowest price – Do you know how much it costs you to make or do what you sell? Selling below this point will result in you losing money. Review costs regularly to make sure any price increases are dealt with. This means developing a mind-set of regularly renegotiating with suppliers, or replacing them; refining processes; increasing prices to customers. Doing whatever is required to cut costs as long as it doesn't negatively impact what your customers value.

Projections/budgets/forecasts – It's no good driving a car looking in the rear vision mirror. You're going to crash. Business is the same. Having a cash flow/budget/projections allows you to look forwards and plan for what may happen (which is easier than reacting after the fact). Use a spreadsheet to anticipate sales and costs for the coming 12 months and make sure your business is going where you want it to. Make any necessary changes now to help fix any problems your projections may show are coming.

Sales – Regularly check your selling price against your lowest price, your competition's prices, and what your customer is willing to pay. You want to make sure your sale price covers costs and anything above that is of value to your customer. If your prices are above competitors, instead of thinking about discounts, think about how you could add more value (for less cost) to improve profits.

Fixed assets – What plant, equipment, vehicles, computers, furniture, fittings, and property do you really need? Can you lease it rather than buy it? Can machinery do the job better/cheaper than employees? Buy new machinery/processes to replace older/slower/more expensive machinery and/or where it improves your process, reduces costs, and adds value to what the customer wants.

Your team – You physically can't do everything yourself – as you grow you will need people to help. What skills do you need to find? Do you need employees or contractors instead? It's very difficult to motivate lazy people so it's a better idea to work with people who are already motivated, enthusiastic and willing to learn. And remember this quote: "hire slow, fire fast".

Store/office – How can you best be where your customers are? Can you lease? Work from your garage? Building up slow is often a good way to limit your costs when starting up a business.

Website – Do you need one? Your website must have a purpose other than just having a website like everyone else. Make sure every page on your website leads your customer to that purpose. Is your website like a store and needs to generate sales? Is your website there to build trust for the customer to contact you? It's not all about being pretty or you telling everyone how good you are – being relevant to your customers on your web pages is just as important as everything else in your business. Make sure everything you say is all about your customer (and not you). And make sure you get a return on what you spend for your web pages – be that new leads/prospects, new customers, or more sales.

Accounting system – You can't manage what you can't measure. You won't know if you're selling your products/services for more than it costs you if you don't have an accounting system to give you the actual numbers. Get one! Preferably an accounting system that your accountant is familiar with or uses themselves (assuming it meets your needs). Use the reports to see how you're going and to make changes where your results aren't going as planned.

Funding – Any debts come with an interest cost which will be an expense and therefore a cost you have to recover. Make sure any loans you get can be covered by sales, and link any loans you do get to the life of whatever it is you are borrowing the money for. For example - if you borrow to pay for machinery that lasts five years, the loan should be for five years as well. Borrow for things that add value to your business – machinery, etc. Try to avoid borrowing to meet costs, and if you do need to borrow, make sure its short term and paid back quickly. Short term flexible facilities have a habit of becoming long term if you're not careful.

Taxes – While taxes are a cost of being in business, you only pay taxes if you make a profit (i.e. are selling for more than your costs). When you don't make a profit, you won't have taxes to pay. That you only need to worry about tax when you make profits, and any tax should come from the profits you make (by allocating a portion of what you get into a tax savings account). And please don't get caught up in the logic I have heard from some accountants and business owners about spending a dollar to save 33 cents tax (which results in you spending 67 cents). By all means look for ways to maximise tax savings when you have to spend some money – but instead of spending money to save tax, look at making a dollar to spend 33 cents tax (and making 67 cents as a result) instead.

Systems/Processes – Automate as much as you can and when you can. Reduce costs and improve profits by using automation and systems/processes where they are cost effective. i.e. the cost of automation/ system/process is less than the results it will bring. Never sacrifice value to the customer for the sake of cost cutting.

When looking at costs in general, think about everything you pay for in terms of an investment rather than a cost. Each and every dollar you spend in your business should add *more* than a dollar to your business. That means you shouldn't spend that dollar on your webpage unless you know your webpage is going to deliver the results you want. When spending your money on anything, please don't get suckered into spending a dollar to make more than a dollar without seeing verifiable proof. This happens a lot in marketing and advertising and in most cases you'll only get back cents in the dollar at best. Promises are meaningless when your business fails.

4

Breaking the Rules

What happens if you break the rules?

You can break one or more of these rules and still survive in business ... but there is a condition. Breaking the rules MUST BE planned – for example:

- You may decide you need to compete with your competitors pricing, or
- Maybe you can strategically price a competitor out of the market by selling at less than cost, or
- You realise you have old stock floating around that isn't so relevant to customers anymore so you sell it at lower than cost to get rid of it and buy more relevant stock, or
- You are investing in new technology and the cost of learning that comes with that.

Just remember that breaking any of the three rules comes with a cost and will never be sustainable in the long run. As long as you don't end up becoming irrelevant to customers, trying to sell at prices your customers won't pay, and selling at prices that are lower than your costs, then your business should be okay.

Part Two

How to Grow Your Business

5

An Accountant's Perspective

As an accountant and a business owner (of my own small accounting firm), I'm exposed to the numerous challenges that any entrepreneur is faced with when starting and then sustaining a business.

I've read countless books about how to grow and develop a business. I've heard many gurus talking both online and on stage about the must-haves and must-dos of business success. And I've read some of the over 430 million responses in Google to the question "How to Grow a Business".

After years of reading, considering, and in some cases applying what I've learnt from books, gurus, and Google, I've come to the conclusion there's a lot of misinformation that:

- Regurgitates what's already out there;
- Deals only with a portion of the whole and fails to take into account business is a complicated system

> with interdependent parts where changing one thing results in something else changing;
> - Was relevant when it was written but won't work today when things are changing so fast.

The problem is *you and I don't have the time to waste* reading information we've read before from elsewhere, or chasing rainbows trying to get the latest business fads working in our businesses, or trying to apply outdated advice that isn't fit for today's world.

We need *less recycling* of existing information and *more* genuinely fresh ideas on how to help us do better and think smarter about succeeding as entrepreneurs.

There's an abundance of *academic thinking* that hasn't been used in the real world. Instead we need examples of things that *have worked* (and better understanding *why* they work) and *how* they can work for someone else.

That's why I started writing books - to share new ways of looking at things with you.

This is NOT a regular business book. It's also not a book about how to make more money, pay less tax, or sell to a wider market. Instead it's a solid overview of what any business owner needs to know and do if they are serious about business growth. Some of it is not pretty. In fact some sections will make you rethink your commitment to your business. But – if you are serious about being successful in any small – medium sized business, then ask yourself if you're ready to *grow* your business.

In this section, you're going to discover:

- A new way of looking at business growth which has nothing to do with growth at all;
- Four mistaken beliefs that may be holding you back and what you can do about them;
- How to build strong foundations in your business to provide a strong platform for growth;
- How to build resilience in your business to weather any significant changes, to survive falls in cash flow, and to allow for further growth;
- Seven ways you can nurture growth in your business;
- Seven things you can do to help sustain growth; and
- Know the symptoms that come from growing too fast (so you can do something about them)

I am going to be straight up with you. You're not going to find any 'magic beans' you can plant to miraculously overnight to find your business growing to the heavens and beyond. You're also not going to find more of the same old information you can get online here. What you will find is a different perspective on growing your business – a perspective built on understanding what's really going on around you and hopefully some 'light bulb' moments you can use to help you grow your business smarter.

Think of it this way – imagine you and I were sitting at a table and I put a coin standing on its edge between us. Each of us can only see one side of the coin. If I asked you what you can see, you would say heads (or tails). If you asked me what I can see, I would say tails (or heads if you see tails). We'd both be right, but we'd also both be wrong.

What's actually in front of us both is a coin with three sides (heads, tails and the bit around the edge). You won't see that unless you know it's a coin, or you change where you're sitting, or you alter the position of the coin itself.

It's a bit like that when it comes to business growth – instead of looking at one side, by understanding some basic truths to business development you will learn that growth can come naturally as long as you have the right 'conditions'.

6

Is it really so hard to grow your business?

The short answer is YES! It is hard. But, the good news is it's easier to grow your business today than it will be in the future.

In New Zealand, businesses are disappearing faster than ever. 36% of businesses born in 2010 with one to five employees ceased to exist by 2014 whether because of bankruptcy, liquidation, mergers and acquisitions, or other causes. Compare that to businesses with one to five employees born in 2001 where only 20% were gone by 2005. That's almost double the death rate in less than ten years.

How can that be? Between 2005 and 2014 we have had greater access to information via the internet as well as faster communication. With so much more readily available information (in most cases that information is available free or at very affordable rates), and quicker access to that information, you would think business owners could learn from others and business survivability should be improving.

I believe that businesses are dying younger and/or faster due to the following reasons:

- The world around us is changing faster all the time. Business environments are now more diverse, dynamic, and interconnected than ever, and far less predictable.
- Business owners are failing to adapt to the growing complexity of their environment;
- Many business owners misread their environment so they end up making the wrong choices about what they should be doing;
- Business owners are overwhelmed by choice.
  - In 2013 there were over 84 documented analytical tools and techniques[1] to choose from to help someone grow a business;
  - there are over 77 million search results in Google about growing your business; and 'experts' everywhere telling us we should try 'X method' because it worked for them.

  The end result leaves business owners paralysed by the fear of picking the wrong strategy and in the end they do nothing.
- Most of the 84 documented analytical tools and techniques are long winded and heavy with business and academic jargon which are hard work for most

---

[1] Analytical tools and techniques were developed by companies and management consulting firms to help provide frameworks for strategic planning. E.g. PEST analysis, Porters five forces, Blue Ocean Strategy …. Strategic planning is just problem solving - setting your business goals, determining the actions you will take to achieve the goals, and organising your resources to accomplish those actions.

entrepreneurs to understand so they end up being avoided;

- Many business owners continue to use 'classic' (dare I say outdated) approaches to growing their businesses; approaches that were designed for when times were very different to today;
- Business owners select the wrong approach to strategy; and
- Business owners fail to support a viable approach with the right behaviours and resources.

So if a business born in 2001 was almost twice as likely to be alive in four years as a business born in 2010, then how can a business born today stand a reasonable chance of growing into the future and not fail?

Is there an easier way to look at growing your business?
I believe the best answers to most questions in life can be found in nature. And looking for a way to grow your business is no different.

When it comes to growth, life itself sets the gold standard. Nature shows us life and death every day in many shapes and forms. Whether its animals, insects, bacteria, or plants – they grow in evolving environments, and are dependant as well as impacted upon by others in the same environment.

Plants have been around much longer than humans (and business). They have had to contend with changing weather, animals and insects coming and going, other plants, and now they have to contend with humans. But yet they still continue to grow.

Businesses have parallels to plants. Plants grow, stall or die depending on the conditions around them (as do businesses).   Plants grow by competing to use what resources they can get to fill whatever space they can (as do businesses).

In nature, a plant cannot grow unless the plant itself is in the right place, at the right time, and it has the right resources it needs. For example:
- A plant's roots and branches must have room (a place) to grow;
- The right time includes when the plant won't be eaten by other insects or animals; and
- Plants need enough sunlight, water and food (resources) in the soil to feed growth.

Your business is no different:
- The right place must allow your business room to expand (e.g. a countries laws, the marketplace;
- The right time includes when your business won't be taken over or beaten by other competitors;
- The right resources include having enough supplies, employees, money, and space to feed your business's growth.

What is different is plants just grow, whereas businesses traditionally think about and target growth. And yet plants win the race against business when it comes to growing and how long they live. There must be something plants are doing right that businesses in general are not.

One of the biggest lessons we can learn from plants when it comes to growing any business is to change how we think about growth. Rather than look at growth as a goal, it's important to consider growth as a result/side effect - something that happens as long as the conditions for your business are right.

Focussing on managing the conditions that are right for your business (or managing your business to be right for the conditions) would mean your business would grow automatically (just like a plant) and there would be no need to 'worry' about achieving x% growth.

As business owners, we have an advantage over plants in that we can 'manage' and adapt our businesses to our conditions, or we can alter our conditions to suit our business. A plant can't do that (not quickly anyway). Any growth (or not) your business achieves will then be a direct result of how well you, and your managers, manage your business and the conditions your business operates within.

7

Changing times call for new ways of thinking

Looking at business growth from the point of view that growth is natural and will happen automatically as long as the conditions are right for your business, is just one way you can make a difference. But when it comes to growing your business, this one change in perspective isn't enough. I have learnt there are at least four more mistaken beliefs that can hold business owners back from reaching their goals:

Stop trying to keep up with change
...instead keep up with the rate of change.

Imagine your competitor is driving a car that is getting faster all the time. You know that it's currently doing 40km/hr. You need to catch up to the car so you put your foot on the accelerator and get up to 40km/hr. The problem is by the time you get up to 40km/hr, your competitors car has continued accelerating and is now doing 60km/hr and getting further away.

You need to be accelerating as fast as (if not faster) than your competitor. If you focus on the speed of your competitor at any one time, then you will never catch them. Instead, try focusing on the pace of change in your competitor's, so you can anticipate where you need to be and accelerate quicker to get *there* first.

Planning is no longer linear (a straight line from point A to point B)
...instead view your business and everything around you as a complex and adaptable system.

Life is too fast and complicated nowadays for you to create plans to get you from point A to point B with supposed incremental stepping stones in between. Your goal (point B) is most likely going to move in the time it will take for you to achieve it. Where you are (point A) is always going to move, and it's going to move in unintended ways as a result of life adjusting to your changes. That will mean the stepping stones you planned between A and B may become irrelevant, you many need new ones, or they may need to shift too. And the longer the period of time between points A and B, the more likely change will get in the way.

Unless you have a more dynamic way of thinking, you may never reach point B, or even worse... if you finally do reach point B you may not want to be there anymore. Viewing things around you as a complex adaptable system means you need to make sure each and every step you take is heading in the right direction.   You can make minor course corrections as you go by constantly re-checking where you are compared to where you want to be. Taking a more fluid approach will allow you to reach your goals regardless of whatever life throws at you.

The economy doesn't have to be great to be able to grow a business

...instead believe your business can grow in any environment (including during a recession) as long as you respect the conditions you are operating in.

Anyone can grow a business when the economy is great. But when a recession hits, poorly run businesses will struggle (or die) because they can no longer hide their faults. Customers become more discerning and will pick other businesses who are more relevant, with better pricing, and who they perceive to be more successful and so likely to be around for longer.

I would argue recessions are the best time to start or grow a business because you're forced to be more relevant to your customers, to offer better prices (I don't mean discounting), and to avoid overspending to remain profitable. It may not be easy, but there are many businesses that grew faster than inflation during a recession (I know because we started Infinite Possibilities in 2008 and have grown at least 10% each year since starting despite the Global Financial Crisis).

There is no one right strategy for business growth

...instead understand it all comes down to matching the right strategy[2] to your 'conditions' at the time.

---

[2] Strategy is the process of determining the actions you will take to achieve your goals, and organising your resources to accomplish those actions.

Contrary to what you may read in books and online, there is no magic formula to growing your business. Each business is unique just like the entrepreneur who starts it, the suppliers the business deals with, the employees, its customers and the environment it functions in. So if everything about your business is unique compared to everyone else, why would you believe anyone when they rave on about how you MUST use 'such and such' strategy because it helped their business grow by over X% last year?

The best way to grow your business is to appreciate certain strategies will be appropriate at certain times. You need to evaluate any strategy against your business to make sure it's appropriate before you consider applying it to your business. You need to pick the right strategy for *your* business at the right time.

8

Building the right conditions for growth

Just like a plant that needs the right conditions to grow, your business will also need the right conditions to grow and reach whatever goals you may have. The right conditions for growth start with having strong foundations and then building up resilience to manage any change that comes from growth.

Strong foundations for growth

One of the conditions that must be right for growing your business is making sure it has strong foundations from which to grow. Think of it like a tree that doesn't have a strong root structure – the tree can be fine while the weather is good, but put any pressure on that tree (like some additional growth or a storm) and the tree's roots are likely to give way and the tree will topple over. That tree will then have to focus on building new and stronger roots before it can grow again.

Your business needs strong foundations, just like a tree. Strong foundations in business terms include:

- Consistently paying all costs (suppliers, employees, bank loans, and other costs);
- Knowing how much tax is due and having the money to pay it; and
- Your business is paying you for your efforts - it may not be what you're worth, but you're getting something.

If these conditions are not right, then whatever growth you were aiming for will stall and you will need to resolve these conditions first to allow for any desired growth.

Building resilience for growth

Once your business foundations are strong, your business should then focus on building up resilience so it can handle the stresses that come from growth. A plant's resilience comes from its ability to weather storms, to survive drought or famine, and to allow for further growth. Your business's resilience is no different.   Your ability to weather any significant changes, to survive falls in cash flow and to allow for further growth, will depend on meeting these milestones:

- Continuing to pay your bills, knowing how much tax you have to pay and having the money put aside to pay it, and paying yourself *something* for your efforts;
- Your business pays you what you're worth;
- Having no overdraft, line of credit, or revolving credit and being current with any term loans;

- Having two months of operating expenses in the bank;
- Paying any after-tax profits as bonuses to your employees to help retain them, and/or to yourself to help you reach your financial goals.

Business owners sometimes make the mistake of taking tax paid profits out of their business before building up any resilience. Taking cash out of your business without building up cash reserves for costs, or paying back overdrafts or lines of credit, means that when times get tough you may find yourself unable to continue.

9

What do you hope to achieve from growing?

A plant's unconscious goals for growth can include sustaining its partners (insects, animals, other plants …) to sustain its own existence. It can include growing large enough to stop other plants stealing its sunlight. It can include getting mature enough to release seeds and grow elsewhere. In business you can have similar goals – sustain your market share; get ahead of your competition and make it harder for them to catch up; create new branches or a franchise to expand your reach.

Without goals, you won't have anything to aim for … and if that's the case then I guarantee that you will achieve that 100% (i.e. you won't get anything).

Your personal goals

Whatever goals you have for the after-tax profits you want from your business, need to be important to *you* - no one else and certainly not your accountant. Think of it this way - instead of saying you want more money from your business, link that to what you want the money for – that trip overseas, a new home, to be able to retire earlier, more time with the family or whatever else rocks your world. These things will have more meaning for you and will help you when things get tough and you need some additional motivation. This is certainly preferable to someone hitting you with a big stick to keep moving.

Setting measurable targets

Regardless of whether you're aiming to achieve the right conditions to allow your business to grow, or to reach some of your personal goals, you can work backwards from what you want to achieve and come up with specific measurable targets you will need to achieve in your business to allow for that desired growth.

Having *specific measurable targets* gives you a way of tracking how you are going, and in doing so, a way for you to make changes as you go so you have a better chance of reaching your goals.

For example, let's say the conditions relating to having strong foundations are in place and you're now building enough resilience in your business to pay for something you've always wanted to do. You want to learn to fly which you know will cost you $1,000 a month and you plan on funding out of your business, which means you can work out the following:

- To get an extra $1,000 a month in your hand, you would have to pay the tax man $500[3], which means you need to 'make' an extra $1,500 a month before tax;
- If you need to make an extra $1,500 a month before tax, you may need to get some additional marketing support. Let's say that will cost you an extra $500 a month in overheads/fixed costs – so now we know you need to make an extra $2,000 a month in gross profit.
- If you need to make an *extra* $2,000 a month in gross profit, and let's say your business has in the past had to sell $2,000 just to make $1,000 gross profit, then your business will need to sell an extra $4,000 a month to get an extra gross profit of $2,000.
- And if you know you need to sell an extra $4,000 a month to get an extra $2,000 gross profit, and you know your average customer usually spends $1,000 a month with you then you know you're either going to find four new customers, or you're going to need your existing customers to increase what they spend and how often they spend with you each month.
- And so on. You look at what you need to achieve, and at what will affect your potential achievements to work out what must be done to reach the objectives you are aiming for. You keep doing that until you can't go any further.

Doing this means you stop aiming for an extra $1,000 in cash a month and instead aim for the right conditions you need

---

[3] Based upon an income tax rate of 33%

that will result in getting an extra $1,000 a month of net profit.

10

Ten ways to nurture growth

Any gardener knows a plant's growth can be altered by playing around with the amount of water, sunlight, fertiliser, and carbon dioxide it gets. A gardener can also alter a plant's growth by how much effort they put into removing or keeping pests away. Business is no different.

Every business has 'levers' that can alter its profitability. A lever is merely one area of a business that is either related to customer numbers, things that when pulled will impact on sales, costs, or cash. And because every business is unique, the impact when pulling one lever for your business may not be the same as any other business.

Knowing which levers you can pull, when to pull them and by how much will help you when planning for growth. Pull the wrong levers by the wrong amount or at the wrong time and your growth will stop or, worse yet, go backwards.

The following ten levers interact together to produce your profit.

The first three levers relate to the number of customers who transact with your business:

1. **Client retention rate** – helps you understand how good your processes are in keeping customers happy and them wanting to continue working with your company. It's important because retaining customers is cheaper, faster, more profitable and easier than attracting new ones.
2. **Leads generated** – are the potential customers who contact you looking for more information about you or what you sell. They may come via your website, telephone, referrals, an event, or advertising.
3. **Prospect conversion** – is your ability to follow up a lead, understand their needs and relate to them, and ultimately help them to buy from you.

The next two levers relate to the sales you gain from your customers:

4. **Transaction value** – is the average dollar amount a customer spends with you within a single transaction. Increase your transaction value by up-selling, bundling, repackaging, adding more value, increasing prices/margins.
5. **Transaction frequency** – is how often a customer purchases from you. You want to encourage people to buy from you more often.

The next lever relates to the direct costs you incur to sell to your customers:

6. **Cost of sales** – Find lower priced suppliers, cheaper raw materials, use labour saving technology, and outsourcing to reduce variable costs, improve efficiency, and save time and resources to improve sales

The next lever relates to the overhead/fixed costs you incur to run your business:

7. **Overheads** – are the fixed costs of running your business – they tend to remain the same regardless of how much you sell. Most businesses can cut administrative expenses up to 10% without affecting their efficiency. Ensure customer relations are not adversely affected, and that costs don't increase in other areas a result of any cuts you make.

And finally, the last levers relate to how you manage your cash in your business:

8. **Debtors Days** – the time taken by your business to convert its credit sales to cash. The easier you make it for your customers to pay you, the clearer your terms are, and the better your process for following up debts, the quicker your customers will pay you and the more money you will have in your bank.
9. **Stock/Work in Progress days** – is the time taken by your business to convert its stock/work in progress into a sale. The quicker you can invoice your customers, the sooner you can get paid. Focus on stock that sells quicker and getting rid of stock that is sitting around wasting space (to use for stock that moves quicker).

10. **Creditors' days** – the average time it takes a business to settle its debts with trade suppliers. Maximise your cash flow by taking as long as possible to pay your bills (within the terms you agreed to).

One problem with using the ten levers is that most businesses know their sales, direct costs, overheads/fixed costs, debtors, stock, creditors because they come from their financial statements which they (or their accountants) prepare come year end. Unfortunately, it's been my experience that most business owners don't have any systems in place that capture information about the number of customers they have, nor the levers behind the sales they achieve - average spend, how many times customers buy from you in a year. Also, the financial reporting by most accountants is done many months after the relevant period you wish to measure and so the information is outdated by the time it's reviewed for planning purposes.

If you don't understand your client retention rate, the leads you generate, your conversion rate, your average transaction value, or transaction frequency, then you will find it harder to achieve growth. It gets harder because you have fewer levers to pull to achieve your growth targets. Fewer levers means greater pressure on the levers you do have and, I don't know about you, but aiming for smaller increases in more levers as opposed to larger increases in fewer levers sounds more appealing and subconsciously easier to achieve.

The power of pulling more than one lever at a time
We know that changing any one lever will result in a certain change in your results. What is useful is finding out that changing more than one lever can result in even greater

change because of the compounding effect of each change. This can be very helpful when you're looking to achieve a large improvement. Instead of having to find a new strategy to achieve a large increase in sales, smaller changes to more than one lever can achieve the same or a better result much easier.

To understand your levers better <u>talk to us about arranging a session to build your own Growth Calculator</u>. Use the growth calculator to look at the real impact on your profitability by making small changes to different activities in your business. It can also help you to work out the areas in your business where the smallest changes lead to the greatest results.

Understanding your levers will allow you to work out which levers you need to pull and by how much to achieve your goals. Then you can then decide on which tactics you will pursue to achieve the desired result.

11

Sustaining Growth

In nature, "if you're not growing, you're dying". It's the same in business too. Things move so fast with new technology, new markets, and new competitors. If you're not continually reviewing and improving your products, services, and business, you are in effect moving backwards and risk your competition overtaking you. So once your business is growing, your next challenge is to sustain that growth.

To sustain growth in your business:

Keep an eye on your foundations

When growing your business, you will want to make sure that your foundations remain strong. For example you need to know your business is continuing to pay its bills, how much tax you have to pay and that you have the money put aside to pay it, and your business is paying you something for your effort ... even if it's not what you're worth). You must also have reporting systems in place to give you the numbers you need to monitor so you can make sure you stay on track and make corrections where needed.

Obey the three golden rules to running any business

- You need to sell a product/service people want to buy; and
- You need to sell your product/service at a price your customers are willing to pay; and
- You need to sell your product/service for enough to make a profit.

Keep an eye on your environment

Just like a plant needs the right environment to grow, so does your business. Trying to grow your business when the environment isn't right will be much harder than when the environment is perfectly set up for what you are planning on doing. Review the political, economic, socio-cultural, technological, legal and environmental factors to make sure there is nothing in the environment that will get in the way of any planned growth both before, and as, your business grows.

Check in with your goals

It will be easier for your business to grow if you've identified the goals you want to achieve from the desired growth. We recommend looking at what you want in your life and then working backwards to find out what your business needs to be achieving to get what you want. Linking your personal goals into what you need from your business will help you to be more motivated to reach your goals if things get rough. If your goals shift, that's okay, just update what your business needs to achieve to help you reach your new goals.

Planning for growth

Will you need additional funding, staffing, training, premises, technology, systems/processes, and outsourcing to manage the planned growth? It's no good aiming for growth and getting it if you can't keep your customers happy. Make sure you don't commit to any extra resourcing until you actually need it, that way your costs won't increase before you need them.

Cash is king

Focus on internal cash funding/financing; use innovative pricing options acceptable to your customers to fund your business growth rather than relying so much on your bank.

Have a trusted adviser and/or accountant

 You need professional help to deal with both starting and growing your business.

Problems with growing?

Focussing on your profit and loss without also keeping an eye on your assets and liabilities is asking for trouble. It is important to manage the working capital (cash, stock/inventory, work in progress, debtors/receivables, and creditors/payables) implications of any growth.

Poorly managed growth can lead to:
- Overtrading - growing your sales faster than you can finance them. This usually leads to enormous accounts payable or accounts receivable and a lack of working capital to finance operations.
- Declining product margins; and
- Expense blowouts.

If this happens, seek help to identify the weak or absent systems in these areas. That will allow you to change or introduce business processes that will improve management controls and therefore performance.

Part Three

Managing Your Tax Easily

13

Accountants and Tax

As an accountant and a business owner (of my own small accounting firm), I'm exposed to the numerous challenges that you may face when it comes to staying on the right side of the tax man.

I've worked with countless business owners helping them with their taxes ... whether that's helping them to find ways to legally minimise their taxes, keeping IRD at bay, or helping business owners navigate the rocky waters of an IRD audit/review/investigation.

Over that time, I've realised that the tax system is a dangerous thing and you really don't have a chance of getting it right because:

- When it comes to tax you're guilty until proven innocent which means the onus is on you to make sure you got it right (which means you need to know all the tax rules relevant to your situation);

- The tax laws are full of jargon which makes it hard to read or understand;
- You can't rely on whatever someone from the IRD tells you because they can be wrong (and that's not a legal defence if it goes to dispute); and
- Other than knowing you have to pay tax (although you might not know how much you have to pay), you are left to your own initiative to learn about the tax requirements you have to meet yourself.

The problem is *you don't have the time to waste* wading through all the tax legislation to understand everything that may be relevant to your businesses. You probably don't have the money to pay tax experts to tell you whether you're doing the right thing tax-wise every time you pay for something. And you also don't want to know you've got a problem once you're at the bottom of a cliff when it's too late – you need to know before you go off that cliff.

You need *more relevant information you can understand and apply in your businesses to help you stay on the right side of IRD. You want more* genuinely fresh ideas on how to help you do better and think smarter about succeeding as entrepreneurs. And you need examples of things that *have worked* (and better understanding *why* they work) and *how* they can work for you.

That's why I started writing books - to share new ways of looking at things with you.

This section is not about how to pay less tax. Instead, it's a solid overview of what any business owner needs to know and do if they are serious about staying on the right side of IRD when it comes to paying your taxes. If you are serious about being successful, then you need to address the issue of tax management sooner rather than later.

This section is especially for you if:

- None of the usual strategies or tools you have tried have worked to help you stay on top of paying the IRD
- You're behind in your taxes and it feels like you're caught in your own personal groundhog day of having to work to pay back the taxman and you don't know how to 'get off'
- You're sick of sleepless nights wondering if you'll have enough to pay the tax man when you need to
- You want a proven way to pay the IRD on time every time

You're about to discover:

- Why timing is everything when it comes to paying your taxes
- Six different cases where timing is an issue
- The key to paying your tax on time every time
- The consequences of not paying the tax man
- A simple and proven way to be able to pay your taxes on time every time
- And some early warning signs something is wrong with your business and what you can do about them if you see them happening to you

What NOT paying your taxes costs you

You should already know that if you're in business and you make a profit then you have to pay tax. Not paying your tax can see IRD chasing you for collection and your debt almost doubling every three years it's not paid. Despite this, not every business pays their tax.

As at June 2015, New Zealand taxpayers owed IRD over $6.1 billion in overdue taxes (excluding child support) of which almost half was for penalties and interest[4]. Of those arrears, 22% was overdue no more than one year, and 54% was older than three years. Paying your tax obviously isn't as easy as it sounds otherwise IRD wouldn't be owed over $6.1 billion in overdue taxes.

In the decades I have worked with small to medium business owners I have noticed many of them fail to understand the need to plan to pay the taxman. We see examples of this each and every year.

Examples like this:

- *Mr P paid the IRD over $1,000 in late filing penalties in one year because he filed his GST returns late. If the GST returns had been filed on time then Mr P would have had an extra $1,000 for something else.*

- *Mr P also paid IRD another $600 because he paid his GST late (not because he couldn't pay it at the time, but because he didn't file his GST returns until they were overdue). That money could have gone towards*

---

[4] Inland Revenue Department Overdue debt by tax type 2006 to 2015

something else if he had paid his GST returns on time.

- *Mr F owed the IRD for taxes in the previous year. He had a payment arrangement with IRD but struggles to meet his commitments. He misses some payments and later catches up. During the year he is reminded of current taxes due this year but he isn't able to pay them when they become due. Any money he gets is going to pay off his arrears in the prior year's first. At the end of the year the prior year's arrears have reduced, but the current year taxes now become overdue which adds to the previous arrears. The end result is his total taxes aren't reducing AND he has paid the IRD $9,379 in late payment penalties and use of money interest over the last three years. That's $9,379 that could have been used to pay current taxes or be spent elsewhere.*

- *Mr H emails us saying "… with a surplus of income over expenses there is fair amount of GST to pay and tax as well. It strikes me that I need to get some more cost into the company and I am wondering about approaches to do that". We met with Mr H and showed him that instead of spending money to save tax and being out of pocket, he should be looking for ways to make more money instead and paying the resulting tax on the resulting increased profits. By all means look for tax savings when you have to spend money that's necessary for your business, but don't spend money just to save tax. That money may be better spent on other things or retained in the business for future investment.*

Every dollar you pay the IRD for late payment penalties, late filing penalties, and interest is a dollar you could have used to reinvest in your business or to enjoy in some other way that means something to you (a night out, a holiday, invest in some further education or just having more fun). I don't know about you, but I'd much prefer to enjoy the money I make in my business than give an extra dollar to the IRD that I didn't need to.

Most business owners understand they have to pay tax if they make money, but what usually happens is that when faced with the choice of paying the taxman at a later date versus paying suppliers or employees 'now', they invariably choose to pay the suppliers and/or employees first and worry about their taxes later. And when 'later' arrives, they simply don't have the money to pay the taxes that are due.

When you fail to treat the taxman as a high priority, you face serious risks such as:

- Losing your business,
- Becoming bankrupt or being liquidated,
- Losing your family home,
- Having to make staff redundant,
- Breaking up with your partner,
- Leaving suppliers and/or staff without the money they were owed, and
- The knock to your ego from failing.

The solution to this may seem quite straightforward: *ensure you have the money to pay your tax when you need to.* Problem solved right? Not quite. Our lives are not that simple and there are many factors that may result in you not being able to pay the taxman when you should.

14

Timing is everything

Come year end, you and/or your accountant work out what your tax liabilities will be. By the time you know what tax how much is payable, you are part way into the next year. If you do need to pay tax, tax on that income won't be payable until sometime later this current year. This is important to understand – the tax payments you pay this year relate to the profit you made in the previous year. There is a one year lag! And it's this 'gap' between when profits are earned and when taxes are paid, that can lead to the following problems:

Forgetting to plan for future tax payments.
Taxes aren't payable every month. On the other hand, suppliers and employees are paid at least once a month.
The problem with this is that you are so busy when you are paying your suppliers/employees every month that you forget to be putting something aside for future tax bills. You mistakenly believe that if there is money in your bank then you can spend it and any surpluses you may have end up

being spent on other things (human nature often dictates you spend what you earn). And when your tax payments finally come up, you may not have enough funds available to pay the IRD5.

Relying on future profits to pay current taxes. You may believe you can pay your future tax payments from future profits ... because if you made a certain amount of profit last year, then surely you will be able to do it again this year. And if that's the case then you can spend what you make this year and don't have to worry about tax until next year.

The problem with this is that it only works as long as your business performs as well next year as it did last year. You get into trouble when you have a good year and then have a bad year and aren't earning the money needed to pay the taxes that are payable for the previous good year.

Expecting your accountant to do it all for you. Being unable to pay the IRD doesn't just happen overnight. It starts the moment you make your first dollar of profit and you don't put something aside to pay the resulting tax that will follow. Business owners sometimes recognise they don't know what they don't know so they get an accountant to help fill in those gaps. However, just getting an accountant isn't enough because not all accountants are created equal.

----

[5] You never want to be on the bad side of the Tax Man. This can be worse than the stereotypical loan sharks you see on television and your life can become very difficult very fast if you are not careful.

There are two problems with leaving it to your accountant to "take care of your taxes" for you:

(i) Your accountant can tell you how much tax you have to pay and when it will be payable, but you still have to run your business and put money aside to pay your taxes. You have to plan for your taxes. If you aren't doing that then your accountant should be explaining to you the need to save/plan for the tax payable in the future, and how best you can do that.

(ii) Your accountant may think they are helping you by simply telling you and later reminding you how much tax you have to pay. They're not! It's not good enough to know what taxes you need to pay if your business can't pay them. You need to know if there is a risk you won't be able to pay the taxes you owe (do you have the savings needed? Is your business making the extra cash needed to cover the tax in the future?). If there are problems you need an accountant who isn't afraid to tell you AND who can help you with specific/practical ideas on what you can do. The sooner you know there are possible problems with being able to pay your tax, the sooner they can be corrected, and the more likely you'll have the time to be able to pay your taxes.

Paying off tax arrears with IRD. When you get behind in your taxes you normally enter into a payment arrangement with IRD to pay those arrears off. One of the conditions of any payment arrangement with IRD is staying current with your current tax obligations.

Paying off tax arrears requires cash. Cash generally comes from making profits. Profits mean more tax. Tax payments are not deductible which means you can't take them away from your income to work out your profit for tax purposes. That means when entering into a payment arrangement with IRD you will have to do better this year than you did last year to cover your existing costs/taxes AND to repay your tax arrears.

Unfortunately most businesses forget about planning for the extra taxes that will arise in the next year that comes from paying off tax arrears this year. If you don't plan for this, then you will pay your arrears back at the expense of this year's taxes leaving you in the same position again next year.

New businesses – New businesses need to be mindful of the "double whammy" of income tax where they end up having to pay two year's tax during their second year in business. For example:

- You start a business in May 2015 and your first tax year ends 31 March 2016.
- You make a profit of $30,000 so there is $8,400 tax to pay.
- In NZ, you will be paying the IRD income tax on 2016 profit on 7 April 2017.
- Depending on when you file your 2016 income tax return with IRD, you may also have provisional tax of $2,940 to pay in August 2016, $2,940 in January 2017 and $2,940 in May 2017 based on 2016 profit.
- If you didn't save any of your $30,000 profit from the tax year ended 31 March 2016, and nothing from your year to date profit for the year ended 31 March 2017, you will need to 'find' $17,220 this year, to be able to pay your 2016 income tax and

2017 provisional tax (you'll be paying two years tax in one calendar year).

If you do not plan for your tax from the first dollar profit you make, you will find having to pay two years tax in one year will be very difficult.

Growing businesses – If you have a business that is constantly growing then you may be able to pay future tax bills (based on prior periods) from future profits. However, this strategy can be risky. I have seen a number of businesses where profits go up and down between years. That means they need to find the money to pay tax this year (based on the previous good year), in a year where there is little or no profit.

You may think that in a bad year there would be tax refunds so what's the problem? That is normally not the case because you only get tax refunds when you overpay tax. In a year of losses there usually is no tax paid so there will be no refunds. More proactive business owners (and/or their accountants) usually estimate their current provisional taxes down to reflect less profit in the current year (when profits are down). But they still need to pay tax this year resulting from when profits were good in the prior year. Paying tax for a prior year, when there is little or no profit in the current year is not easy.

Recognising the problems that can arise from the gap between when you earn income and when you pay tax on that income is just the first step in getting ahead. The next step is in taking ownership of your business and paying your tax as opposed to blaming others.

Not paying your Tax is simply bad planning

I have met many accountants and business owners who will blame everyone and everything but themselves when they can't pay their taxes. For example, in the years following 2008 it has been common to hear business owners blame their lack of money on the Global Financial Crisis.

I don't accept that for a second. I accept the Global Financial Crisis impacted some businesses and what was in their bank accounts. However it wasn't the Global Financial Crisis's fault that those same businesses couldn't pay their tax. I believe business owners (and their professional advisers) were to blame for:

- Not planning or managing the tax that was due;
- Not identifying being unable to pay the taxman until it was too late (there are signs this would be a problem before it ever became a problem);
- Ignoring the Three Golden Rules of Business – staying relevant to customers, selling at a price customers are willing to pay, and selling at a price above costs to make a profit.

In reality, not being able to pay the taxman should never be a problem... ever!

Paying tax is no different than having to pay suppliers or employees. It's just another cost of doing business. The only real difference is that the taxman usually gets paid less frequently than employees or suppliers ... which means you need to plan for this. If you can't pay the taxman today for any income tax or GST on what you sell then you probably have a bigger problem with your business that really needs to be looked at.

The consequences can hurt – a lot!

Maybe it's because people generally dislike the tax man, or maybe it's because business owners as a whole don't have as close a relationship with the IRD as they do with their employees or suppliers. Whatever the reason, business owners seem to think it's okay to pay employees and/or suppliers before they pay their taxes.

Not paying the taxman is a serious decision with serious outcomes. Currently[6] non-payment of the IRD will result in the following charges:

- An initial 1% late payment penalty the day after the due date;
- A one off 4% late payment penalty one week later;
- A 1% late payment penalty every month thereafter;
- Use of money interest, currently at 8.7% per annum; and
- Depending on the type of tax involved, there can be further or higher penalties for non-payment.

This equates to a finance cost of at least 28% in the first year and 23% every year thereafter. At these kinds of rates, your original taxes payable can double every three to four years. To be fair, IRD can negotiate payment arrangements with taxpayers to settle their arrears but you will still be charged interest and any initial penalties leading up to the commencement of any agreed payment arrangement.

---

[6] I say currently because there is an IRD discussion document issued by the IRD talking about removing the late payment penalties on income tax for unpaid provisional tax.

The IRD does not like to be treated as a bank by taxpayers. Therefore, when you don't pay the IRD you will attract IRD's attention as IRD commences collection proceedings in an effort to collect what it is owed. We prefer to avoid attracting IRD's attention because once you get on the wrong side of IRD, life can become a lot harder than it needs to be.

15

The best way to plan for tax

Start saving for tax by using a tax savings account
The simplest solution is to have a tax savings account where you put money into it on a regular basis and that money is used solely to pay your income tax and GST to the IRD. If you're about to start a business then you use your tax savings account from day one. If you have been in business for a while and you aren't using a tax savings account then you need to go to your bank and start using one today.

My recommendation is to put the necessary amount aside every month so you're not wasting too much time on this during a month. However there is nothing stopping you if you want to do this daily or weekly if you prefer. Most good accounting systems should be able to tell you how much sales you banked in a specific time period so it should only take a few minutes to work out what you should be transferring to your tax savings account and then go online and make it happen.

Putting aside a percentage of sales each month will 'protect' you whether business is good or bad. In a good year you will need to put more aside; in a not so good year, you might have to plan for less tax. In either case, as long as the percentage you put aside is close to the actual tax payable, it should be enough to cover your tax obligations.

Putting aside a certain percentage of the income you bank every month will never be perfect. You may well have a bit extra you don't need, or you may need to find extra funds to settle the final bill. But it's easier to find a few thousand to square things up with IRD than having to find tens of thousands if you didn't put anything aside at all.

If you don't trust yourself to use the tax savings account solely to pay your taxes, then there is nothing stopping you from making voluntary GST or income tax payments to IRD as you go, rather than saving that money yourself. IRD will certainly not complain if you pay them early.

Personally I prefer to be earning interest on my money until I have to pay the IRD rather than letting the taxman earn that interest on *my* money paid early – I mean why should IRD get the interest benefits? Your choice will be based on how confident you are that you will only use a tax savings account to pay the IRD and not use those funds to pay suppliers or employees (or yourself).

How much should you be saving each month?
If you need to be transferring a certain percentage of the income you bank every month, then the obvious question is "how much?" The answer to that question is "it depends". Every business is different, with different:
- Mark-ups on costs,
- Structures of direct costs versus overheads, and

- Profit margins.

Businesses with a trading history

When you have a business that has been trading for a while, the way we work out the percentage of sales you should transfer to cover your tax obligations is to start with how much tax you had to pay the taxman for the last year for income tax, student loans, working for families and GST and compare that to the sales you banked for that same year.

For example:

Item[7]	$	%
Sales banked (actual amount banked into bank account – incl GST)	407k	
GST payable for 1 April to 31 March in same year	30k	7.3%
Company Income tax payable for 1 April to 31 March in same year	13k	3.2%
Personal Income tax payable for 1 April to 31 March in same year	30k	7.3%
TOTAL tax savings needed per month (rounded up).	73k	17.8%

In this example 18% (rounded up) of sales banked each month needs to be transferred into your tax savings account

---

[7] All tax amounts are the tax payable in the same period the sales relate to. i.e. for the year ended 31 March 2016 you would include the GST return payment/refund for the period ended 31 March 2016 even though it was paid/refunded in April/May 2016. The same applies for Income Tax – use the tax payable before deducting provisional tax payments – this is the tax payable for the year and what you need to fund to be able to pay provisional tax and/or any final terminal (square up) tax.

each month and that will cover any income tax or GST payments to IRD for you and your company.

New businesses

If you are just starting a new business, then you won't have a history of income and tax payments to be able to calculate your tax savings percentage. Instead, you should refer to your budget/projections for the expected amounts for each item to work out your tax savings percentage. If you don't have a budget/projection then you should consider preparing one or talking with your accountant to prepare one.

Annual review

The percentage you should save will change as your business structure and margins change, and/or if the tax rates change. We recommend you recalculate the percentage you put aside for tax savings whenever you make any significant changes to your business structure or margins (or at least once a year) so that it stays up to date.

Adjustments

Fixed Assets bought or sold - sometimes, your GST payable in a year may include asset purchases or sales. If they are significant and/or they won't happen again next year, we would normally adjust the GST payable amount for the year by taking out the GST impact for the assets bought or sold.

Cash versus accrual basis GST – you might want to consider using sales revenue as opposed to sales banked if you are on an invoice basis for GST (i.e. you account for GST when you earn a sale and not when you receive the money for that sale). It shouldn't make much of a difference if your debtors are consistent with your sales.

Increasing debtors/accounts receivable – if your debtors are increasing faster than your sales or sales banked, you should consider using sales earned as opposed to sales banked to make sure you are saving enough for tax (or alternatively get your debtors to pay you so you don't end up paying taxes on income you have earned but haven't received).

How much should you have in your tax savings account?

The balance held in your tax savings account on any date should be the amount you need to pay the IRD for GST and income tax if you had to close your business down on that same date. This includes past year taxes AND taxes on year to date profits.

You can work out how much you should have in a tax savings account if you had to pay the taxman 'today' by adding up:

    i.   any tax payable or refunds less payments for the most recent year end;

    ii.   GST owing to date; and

    iii.   any tax payable/refundable on your profit to date.

For example: let's say I am working this out as at 30 June 2016 for a business with a 31 March balance date:

GST owing to 30 June 2016	$500
Personal/company/trust income tax payable for 1 April 2015 to 31 March 2016	$6,000
Personal/ company/trust income tax payable and student loan for 1 April 2016 to 30 June 2016	$7,500
Less 2017 provisional tax paid to IRD by 30 June 2016	$nil
Tax savings balance should be	$14,000

If there is more than $14,000 in your tax savings account then you could remove the difference to business savings. If there wasn't enough, then you would consider topping up your tax savings account for the difference from business savings, or putting a plan into action to make sure you make up the difference needed before it's too late.

16

Get help from your accountant

If any of the following apply to you then I highly recommend you talk with your accountant:

- You need help working out what you need to be saving for tax each month; or
- You do not have the funds in your bank account to get the initial amount needed into your tax savings account; or
- You have arrears owing to IRD for prior years which also need to be paid.

If all your accountant is doing is telling you *what* tax you need to pay, and possibly helping you with arranging a payment plan with IRD, then we would suggest you look for a more proactive accountant. A good accountant should be able to:

- Learn how much you should be saving to cover your taxes;

- Highlight to you if you don't have enough currently set aside to pay the tax that would be due today if you closed your business;
- Create a plan to get up to date with your taxes;
- Help you plan for any tax payments you need to make;
- Negotiate with IRD or your bank to arrange a payment plan to get up to date with your taxes;
- Show you how you can save on taxes on necessary business costs;
- Show you how to run your business so you cover your taxes;
- Show you how to grow your business to do even better; and
- Warn you about anything you may be doing that could risks attracting IRD's attention.

Are there any challenges/issues you need to be aware of?
As is the case with everything in life, there may be times when following our advice seems impossible. That's alright. We've been there before so we know the things life may throw at you and what you can do about it.

Not having enough money
When transferring a percentage of your income each month to a tax savings account, you may find yourself facing one or more of the following situations:

(a) You cannot transfer the required percentage for the month from your business accounts into your tax savings account;

(b) You cannot pay a supplier or an employee what they are due, and you are considering using the money in your tax savings account to pay them; or

(c) You cannot pay the required tax from your savings
     account.

In each of these cases, there is likely to be a problem with
your business. This can indicate any or all of the following:

- You may not have sold enough, or
- Your profit margins are slipping, or
- You have had too many overheads that month, or
- Your customers are using you like a bank and paying you too slow, or
- You are paying your suppliers too quickly, and/or you aren't taking advantage of payment terms your suppliers could give you, or
- You are holding onto stock/inventory that you really need to get rid of (even if it's not at retail prices), or
- You aren't invoicing your customers quickly enough, or
- The percentage you are saving for tax is wrong.

Believe it or not this is GREAT NEWS! Realising you have a
problem in your business now means you have time to fix it.
Most business owners don't see they have a problem until it
hits them over the head and by then it's normally too late to
do anything about it except limit the damage.

Whatever the reason, NOW is the right time to take a closer
look at your business (with your accountant?) to work out
what is happening and to make some changes so it doesn't
happen again. Ignoring these warning signs now only puts
your business at risk, and/or increases the cost to you in time
and money to resolve them properly later.

Getting enough tax savings to get started

Sometimes it can be difficult to catch up on arrears owing to IRD, and/or getting that initial amount needed to be able to pay the IRD if you were to close your doors. In these cases what we recommend is to add an additional percentage to the monthly tax savings to help 'catch-up'.

To work out what that additional percentage is requires balancing the following:

- What you/your business can afford;
- The amount you are in arrears with IRD;
- Existing payment arrangements you need to honour (or renegotiate?) with IRD; and
- How much you need to top up your tax savings account to get up to date.

We would normally have a meeting with you to discuss these issues with you to ensure you achieve the best result for you (a result you can achieve).

- A possible payment arrangement with IRD, and
- Reviewing your business to ensure it can afford its tax obligations.

Having a good accountant who can help you to balance all these needs will go a long way to helping you regain control of your business (and life).

Conclusion

IRD will investigate taxpayers who have not paid their taxes. If you want to avoid being someone the taxman is looking at, then you need to pay your taxes *when* they fall due. One way you can do that is by making sure you view your tax obligations like any other cost of doing business and put enough away each month into a tax savings account from which you pay the IRD.

If you already have the Tax Man looking at you then you will need a plan to get back up to date with your tax payments. Your plan may include:
- Monthly savings,
- A top up for any arrears,
- A possible payment arrangement with IRD, and
- Reviewing your business to ensure it can afford its tax obligations.

Having a good accountant who can help you to balance all these needs will go a long way to helping you regain control of your business (and life).

Next Steps

Knowing the Three Rules of running any business, how to grow your business and planning for tax is just the beginning when it comes to starting or growing a business.

If you're serious about starting your business, getting more from your business, or managing your taxes better, you can access our incredibly useful FREE resources in our Learning Zone on our website, www.infinitepossibilities.co.nz/news

If you'd like our help getting your business started successfully, getting more out of your business, or getting on top of your taxes, then visit our 'Services' page on our website for options. www.infinitepossibilities.co.nz/services

If you're curious about what happened with my daughter and her first apple business... she got distracted by something else "bright and shiny" and our Apple trees didn't have as much fruit as they have had in the past so it didn't happen. I haven't given up though because she did learn the Three Rules and I believe it's good for her to learn about having your own business (even at this young age). There's always next year ☺

About Brydon Davidson

Not your 'typical accountant'!
In fact, if you really want to make Brydon Davidson feel bad, refer to him *as 'just another accountant'* because he strives to be *more than 'just another accountant'*.

For years he's railed against the system that enables entrepreneurs to work with accountants who are still operating in much the same fashion as they have for hundreds of years. You know the ones who talk about their services more than they listen to your needs; are reactive to your needs instead of being proactive business partners; look backwards at your financial history instead of forwards to your future planning, and worst of all they use too much jargon and *'accountantese'* like English is their second language.

Brydon started Infinite Possibilities in 2008 because he wanted to approach delivering his professional services differently. Sure – his company does the required reporting, filing, and financial aspects of accounting services, but that's where the similarity to traditional accountants ends.

Equipped with a high intellect, an insatiable curiosity and an extremely logical and detailed mind – Brydon likes things to make sense, enjoys solving problems (the more complex the better), strives to always do the "right" thing (in every sense of the word), and constantly works to find better ways of achieving results by applying common sense to small business models.

Not content with knowing facts and figures, he studied coaching for one year, then set about learning everything he could through establishing his own small business practice, working with coaches, and delving fully into the world of online learning and marketing.

His services extend to how to set up of your business, how to grow your business, how to optimise your taxes, and how best to use companies and trusts so that you're not throwing good money after bad with poorly set up structures.

Brydon lives in Hamilton, New Zealand with his wife and daughter, and his beloved patch of fruit trees.

Infinite Possibilities

Accounting as it should be

At Infinite Possibilities, we believe that anything is possible. The only *real* limitation to anything in life and business is in our minds. Just about everything comes down to believing it's possible, knowing what your options are, making some choices, and then doing something about it. And that's what we do. We work with our clients to help discover what you really have, what you want (or need) to get, and the options available to get there (which bits you could add and/or take away). We'll then help you make some choices and guide you through what you need to do.

Start Your Business:
We can help you get started and build a solid foundation for your business where:
- Your business is paying its own costs;
- You know how much you owe in taxes throughout the year and you're setting aside money to pay your taxes on time; and
- You're getting something back for your effort (even if it's not necessarily what you're worth yet); so

- You'll have a higher probability of success and avoid becoming one of the many businesses that fail within their first three years

Grow Your Business:

We can help you build up resilience and then get more from your business where your business will:
- Continue to pay all its costs, including taxes;
- Be paying you what you're worth for your effort;
- Not have to rely on overdrafts, revolving credits, or credit cards and will be current on any term loans;
- Have at least two months of operating expenses saved in the bank; and
- Be able to pay you or your team more so you can all enjoy more of those special moments in life.

When it comes to growing your business, our ultimate goal is to help you achieve better results than you were getting before asking for our help.

Manage Your Tax:

Get on top and stay on the right side of IRD where:
- You will know how much tax you have to pay;
- You'll be up to date with the taxes you owe IRD;
- You will be filing all your returns with IRD on time;
- You'll be paying the IRD on time, every time; and
- You won't be paying more tax than you have to.

Protect Your Assets

We can help you improve the chances of keeping what you have by:
- Making sure you have and are using the right structures

- Ensuring you're not doing anything that may risk you losing what you have
- Improving your chances of keeping whatever you have if the unexpected happens

Check out our other titles on Amazon:
- Grow Your Business - *Seven Steps to Building a Strong Foundation, Plus Resilience for Sustainable Growth*
- 3 Golden Rules for Running Your Business – *Critical Business Rules for Any Business From Start Up to Empire*
- Manage Your Taxes – *Tax Planning Essentials for Small Business Owners*
- Protect Your Assets – *Good Trusts vs Bad Trusts and Keeping What You Have*

For more information on how you can, Start and/or Grow Your Business, Manage Your Taxes and Protect Your Assets be sure to check out our free learnings which are available on our website. www.InfinitePossibilities.co.nz

If you would like our help with starting your business, getting more from your business, staying on the right side of IRD, or keeping what you have, be sure to ask us about our Breakthrough Sessions.
www.InfinitePossibilities.co.nz/breakthroughs

Locating Us
Infinite Possibilities Ltd
Unit 14, Chartwell Professional Suites
9 Lynden Court, Chartwell
HAMILTON 3210
New Zealand

Phone: (07) 853 6527
Email: info@infinitepossibilities.co.nz
Skype: infinite.possibilities.nz

Postal Address:
PO Box 12274 Chartwell
HAMILTON 3248, New Zealand

A Note of thanks from the author

"If I have seen further than others, it is by standing on the shoulders of giants" Isaac Newton

Where I am today, the lessons I have learned, what I have shared in this book, and how I think has been the direct result of others around me. I know I wouldn't be who I am today without their contribution to my life. I want to express my gratitude to the people who saw me through this book; to all those who provided support, talked things over, read, wrote, offered comments, and assisted in the editing, proofreading and design:

A huge thank you to Maria Carlton for her incredible patience dealing with my never ending questions about publishing this book; her encouragement and support in believing I had something of value I should share with other business owners; and her above and beyond assistance in getting this book published.

I would like to thank my wife, Anastasia Hildred who supported and encouraged me in spite of all the times my business and writing (and publishing this book) has taken me away from her and our daughter in recent years. I look forward to returning that support in the coming years.

I want to thank Dennis Johns for his support getting my accounting business started and helping me deal with a number of business lessons I didn't know how to deal best with at the time. I don't know where I would be if my business had failed without his help.

Chrissy McCracken is owed my gratitude for helping me better understand how I think and what I think, and helping me become more aware of both myself and the world in general. Being able to explore my own thinking, both the good and the bad, is enlightening.

To my clients, thank you for agreeing to let us work with you, allowing me the opportunity to help you do better, and trusting me with your business and lives. We don't always get it right (the price of living infinite possibilities and looking for newer/better ways of doing things) so I really appreciate it when you give us the chance to make it right.

I want to acknowledge the following who I know have added to my learning. Specifically:
- Henry Ford, Richard Branson, Bill Gates, and Steve Jobs who all dared to be different, who never settled for mediocrity, and who challenged the status quo when the world around them couldn't see what they could. Just because it's always been done this way, doesn't mean it should.

- Verne Harnish, TED Talks, Simon Sinek, Trent Taylor, Rob Nixon, Kevin Rogers, Dale Crosby (and many others) whose books, articles, blogs, talks, webinars, videos, audio books, and courses all contributed to the frameworks and ideas I now share with others both in my business and this book.
- Mark Jenkins, the GAP 2014 Ltd and 2020GC's for their support in growing my business development knowledge which contributed to the writing of this book.

Last and not least, I ask forgiveness of all those who have been with me through the journey to here and whose names I have failed to mention.

Brydon Davidson